FATHER'S EASY ANSWERS

TO LIFE'S DIFFICULT QUESTIONS

HEATH HARMISON

The opinions and views expressed herein belong solely to the author and do not necessarily represent the opinions or views of Cedar Fort, Inc. Permission for the use of sources, graphics, and photos is also solely the responsibility of the author.

ISBN 13: 978-1-4621-2341-4

Published by Plain Sight Publishing, an imprint of Cedar Fort, Inc.
2373 W. 700 S., Springville, UT 84663
Distributed by Cedar Fort, Inc., www.cedarfort.com

Library of Congress Control Number: 2018963407

Cover design and interior layout by Sarah Wakefield
Cover design © 2019 Cedar Fort, Inc.
Edited by Kathryn Watkins and Kaitlin Barwick

Printed in Canada

10 9 8 7 6 5 4 3 2 1

Printed on acid-free paper

FATHER'S
EASY ANSWERS
TO LIFE'S DIFFICULT QUESTIONS

Dedicated to all the fathers out there who choose to love and be playful with their children—to not just be a "father" but also a "dad." And to my own dad for teaching me the value of working hard and having a sense of humor.

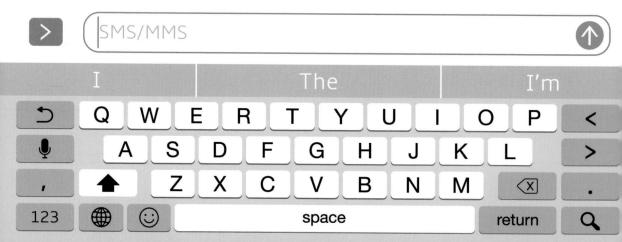

how old are you?

under 10

over 10

you're never too old for cartoons!

SHOULD I BUY

FLOWERS

FOR MY WIFE?

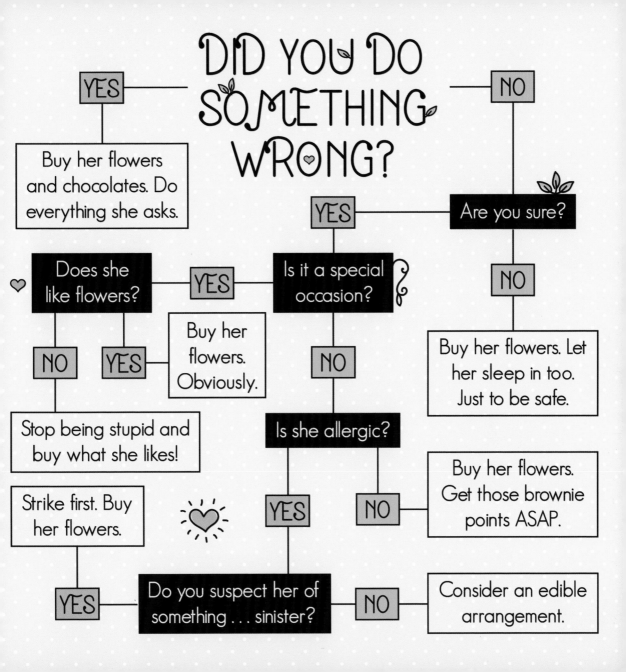

DOES MY CHILD ACTUALLY NEED A BAND-AID?

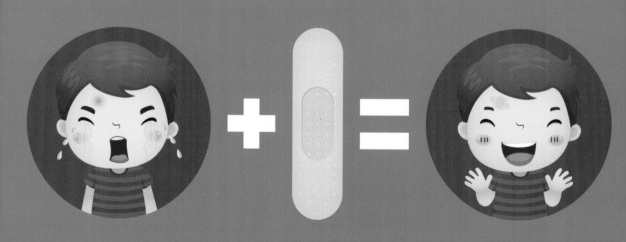

SHOULD I GRILL TONIGHT?

GRILL MENU
· BURGERS · STEAKS ·
· KEBABS · CHICKEN ·

★ DAD: GRILL MASTER ★

BBQ

SHOULD
I LET MY
kids stay up?

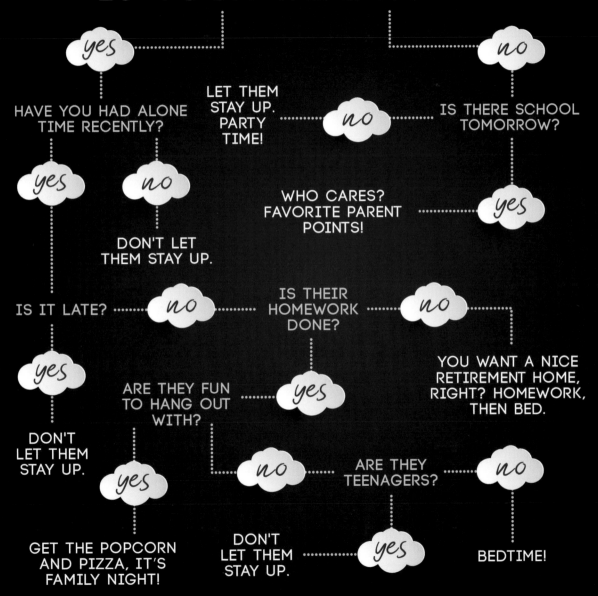

SHOULD I

PURCHASE

A SHINY NEW BOAT

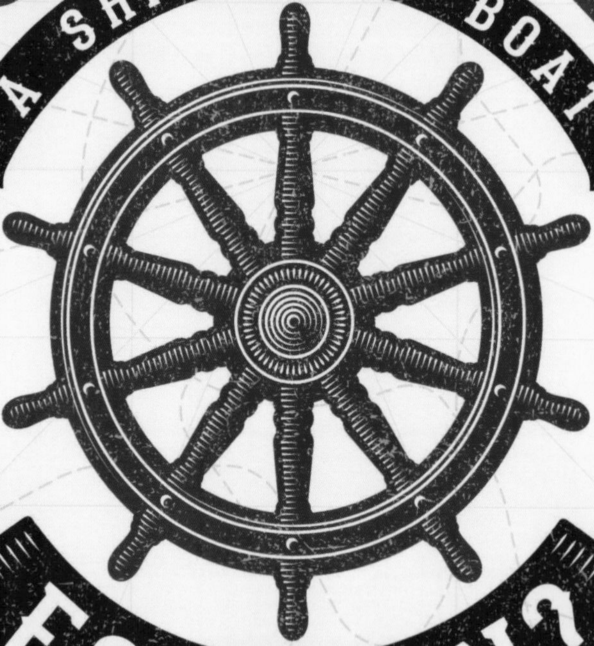

WEST

EAST

FOR FUN?

DO YOU LIVE NEAR WATER?

MAYBE JUST WATCH AN OCEAN DOCUMENTARY. — **NO**

YES — ARE YOU PREPARED TO WASTE MONEY? — **NO**

A BOAT IS PERFECT FOR YOU! — **YES**

JUST BORROW IT FROM THEM. WIN-WIN. — **YES** — DO ANY OF YOUR FRIENDS OWN A BOAT?

MAYBE STICK WITH A JET SKI. — **NO**

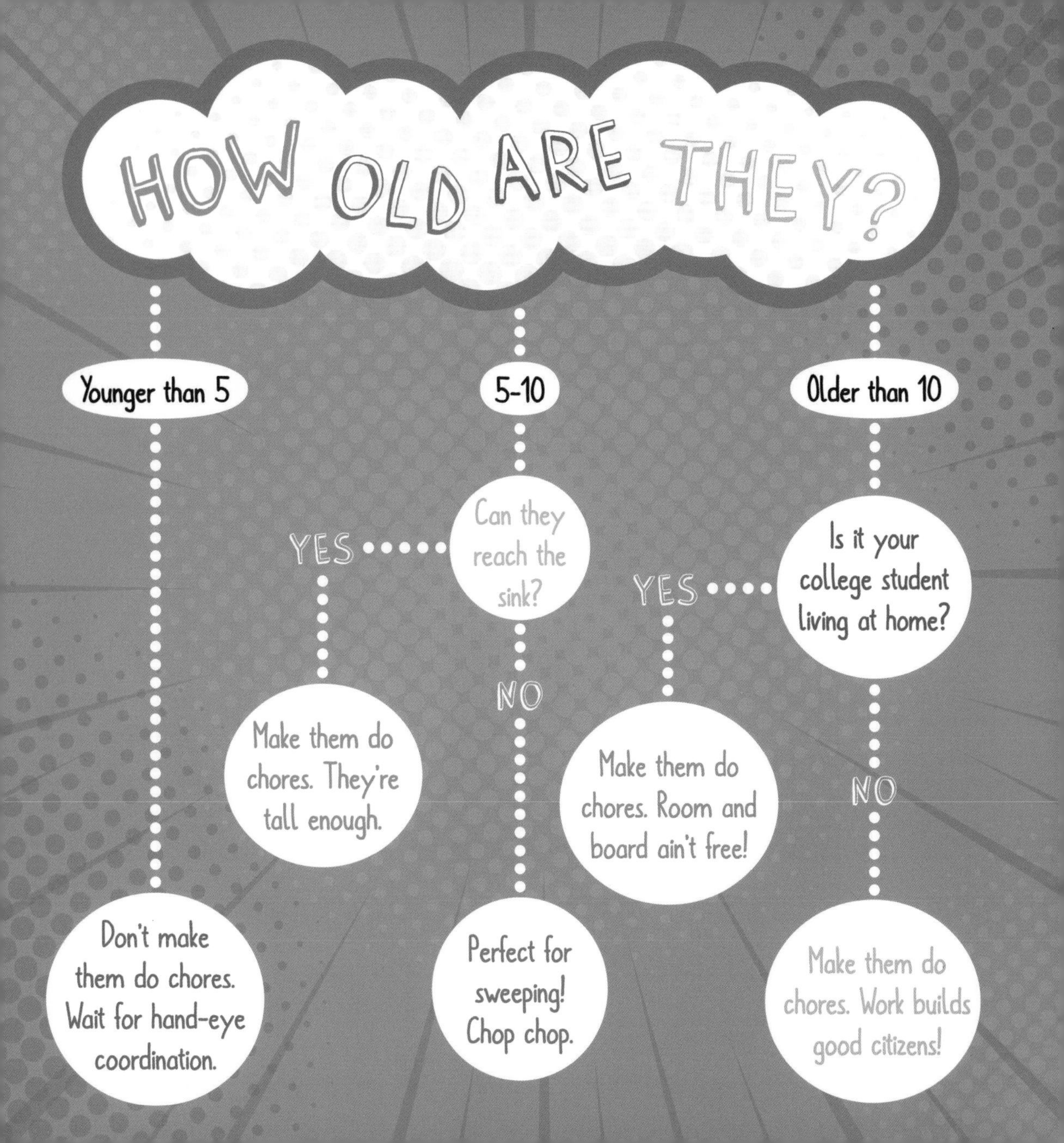
HOW OLD ARE THEY?
Younger than 5
5-10
Older than 10
Can they reach the sink?
YES
Make them do chores. They're tall enough.
NO
Perfect for sweeping! Chop chop.
Don't make them do chores. Wait for hand-eye coordination.
Is it your college student living at home?
YES
Make them do chores. Room and board ain't free!
NO
Make them do chores. Work builds good citizens!

Should **I KEEP EATING?**

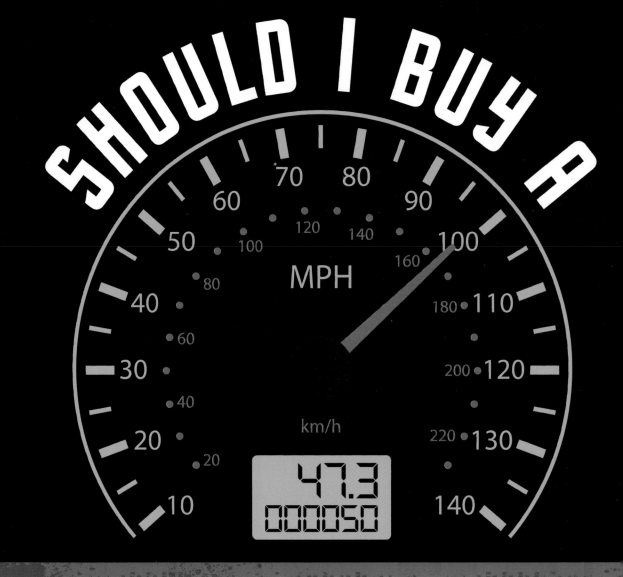

SHOULD I BUY A

MPH

km/h

NEW CAR?

DOES YOUR WIFE KNOW

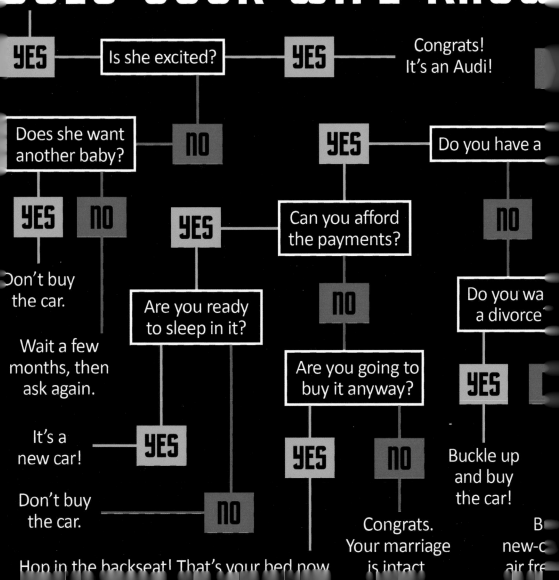

YES — Is she excited? — **YES** — Congrats! It's an Audi!

Does she want another baby? — **no**

YES **no**

Don't buy the car.

Wait a few months, then ask again.

It's a new car!

Don't buy the car.

YES — Are you ready to sleep in it? — **YES**

no — Hop in the backseat! That's your bed now

YES — Can you afford the payments?

no — Are you going to buy it anyway?

YES —

no — Congrats. Your marriage is intact

YES — Do you have a

no — Do you wa a divorce

YES — Buckle up and buy the car!

B new-c air fre

SHOULD I LET MY WIFE DO IT?

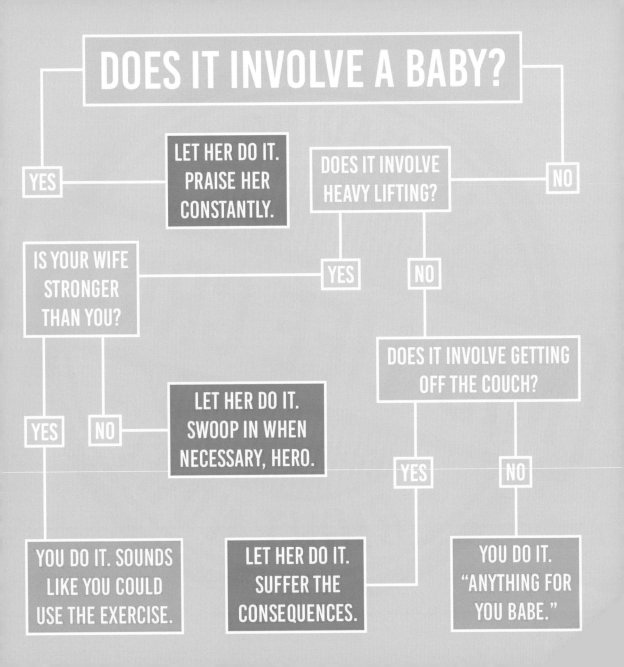

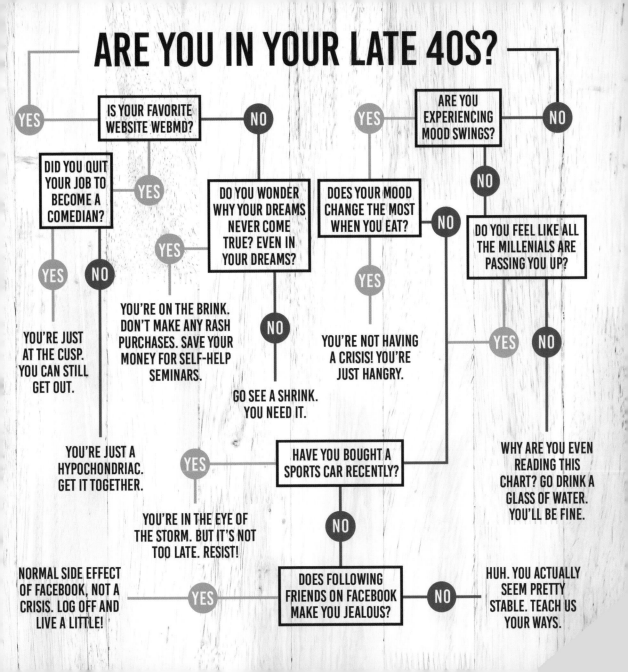

SHOULD we ViSit the IN-LAWS?

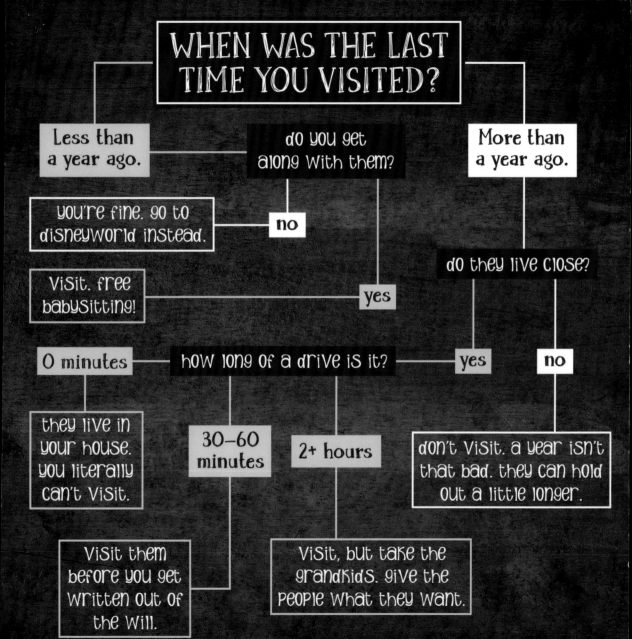

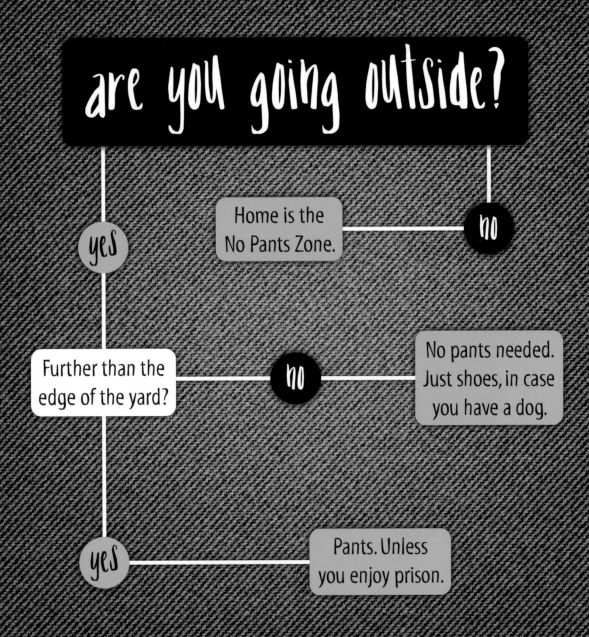

Should I host a ✕✕✕

SUPER
BOWL
PARTY?

30   40   5

IS YOUR TEAM PLAYING?

yes → Does your wife like football? → **no**

yes

Do you like the same team?

yes ← Do you like the same team?

Host the party.

no ← Are you prepared to sleep on the couch over the outcome?

Abort! Don't host a party.

Host the party. Set her up with a girls' day.

yes → You're a true fan. Host the party.

Don't host. Make one of them do it. ← **yes**

Do your friends like it? → **no**

no ← Do you like football? ← **no**

yes → Do you like cooking?

no → Try a D&D party instead. But ask your mom first.

yes

Host the party. ← **yes** ← Do you have a good TV and sound system?

Don't host. Make yourself 5 pounds of wings and eat it all. ← **no**

no

Maybe just go to a sports bar.

40   30

DO I HAVE TO GO TO WORK?

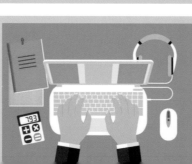

ARE YOU A MILLIONAIRE?

YES

PFFT! "WORK." YOU MEAN HANG OUT ON YOUR YACHT?

NO

DO YOU WANT TO BE?

YES

THAT'S THE SPIRIT! GO BUY A LOTTERY TICKET ON YOUR WAY TO WORK.

NO

YOU'VE GOT GUTS. BUT YOU'RE LATE FOR YOUR SHIFT AT WALMART.

SHOULD I START A ROCK BAND?

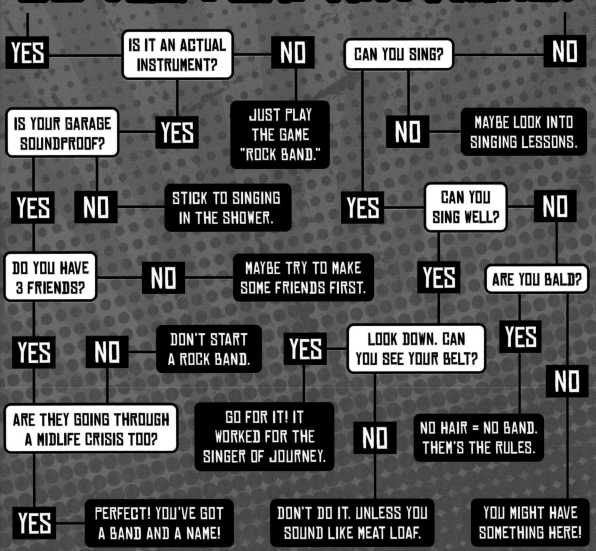

Should I call a

BABY SITTER?

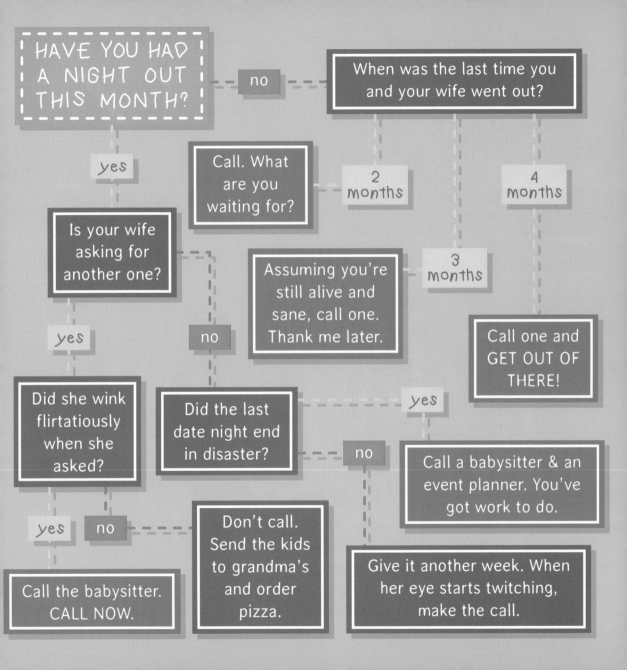

IS MY **WIFE** iN **LABOR?**

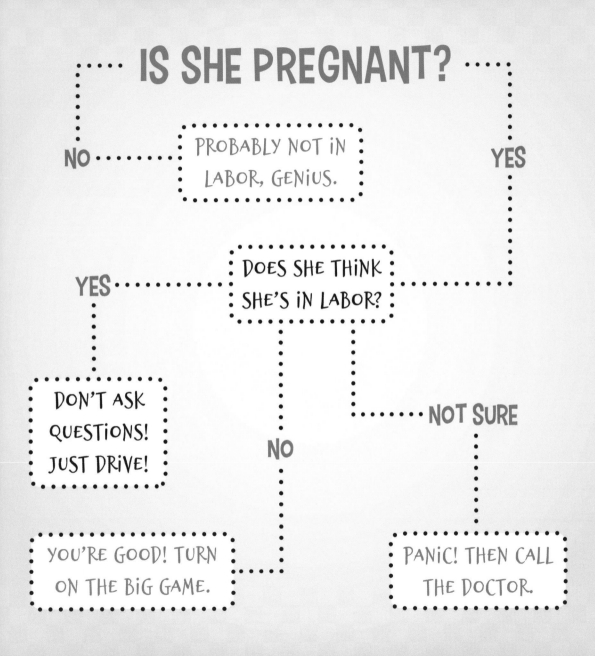

Should I

LET MY TEENAGER

TAKE THE CAR?

DO YOU WANT A NEW CAR?

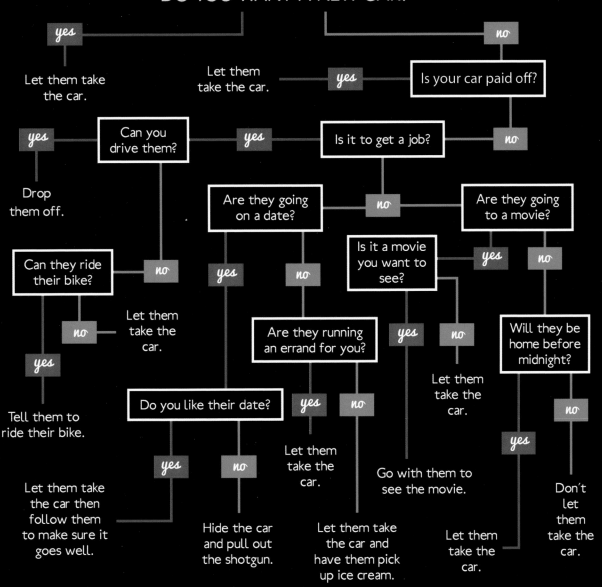

Should I give my kids Ice Cream?

CAN I EAT A BITE OF MY WIFE'S FOOD?

IS SHE PREGNANT?

YES — IS SHE PREGNANT? — **NO**

YES → Does she have a fork in hand? → **YES** → Don't touch it.

Does she have a fork in hand? → **NO** → Can you outrun her? → **NO** → Don't touch it.

Can you outrun her? → **YES** → Take it and run!

Is she on a diet? → **YES** → Don't touch it. Diet food tastes like dirt.

Is she on a diet? → **NO** → Do you wanna live? → **YES** → Don't touch it.

Do you wanna live? → **NO** → Savor it. That's your last meal.

SHOULD I MAKE THE
KIDS
DINNER?

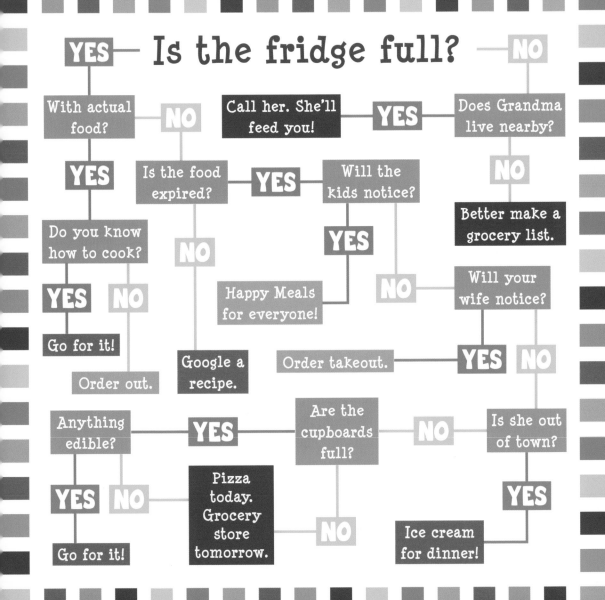

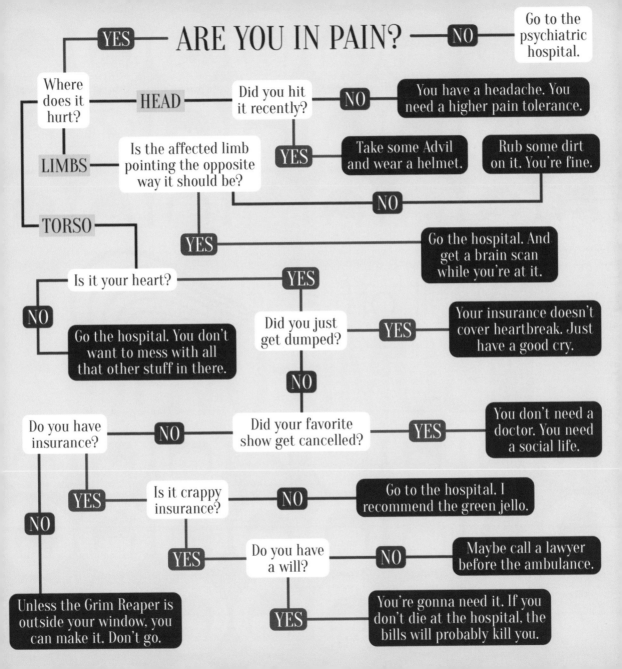

CAN I Pull off a COMB-OVER?

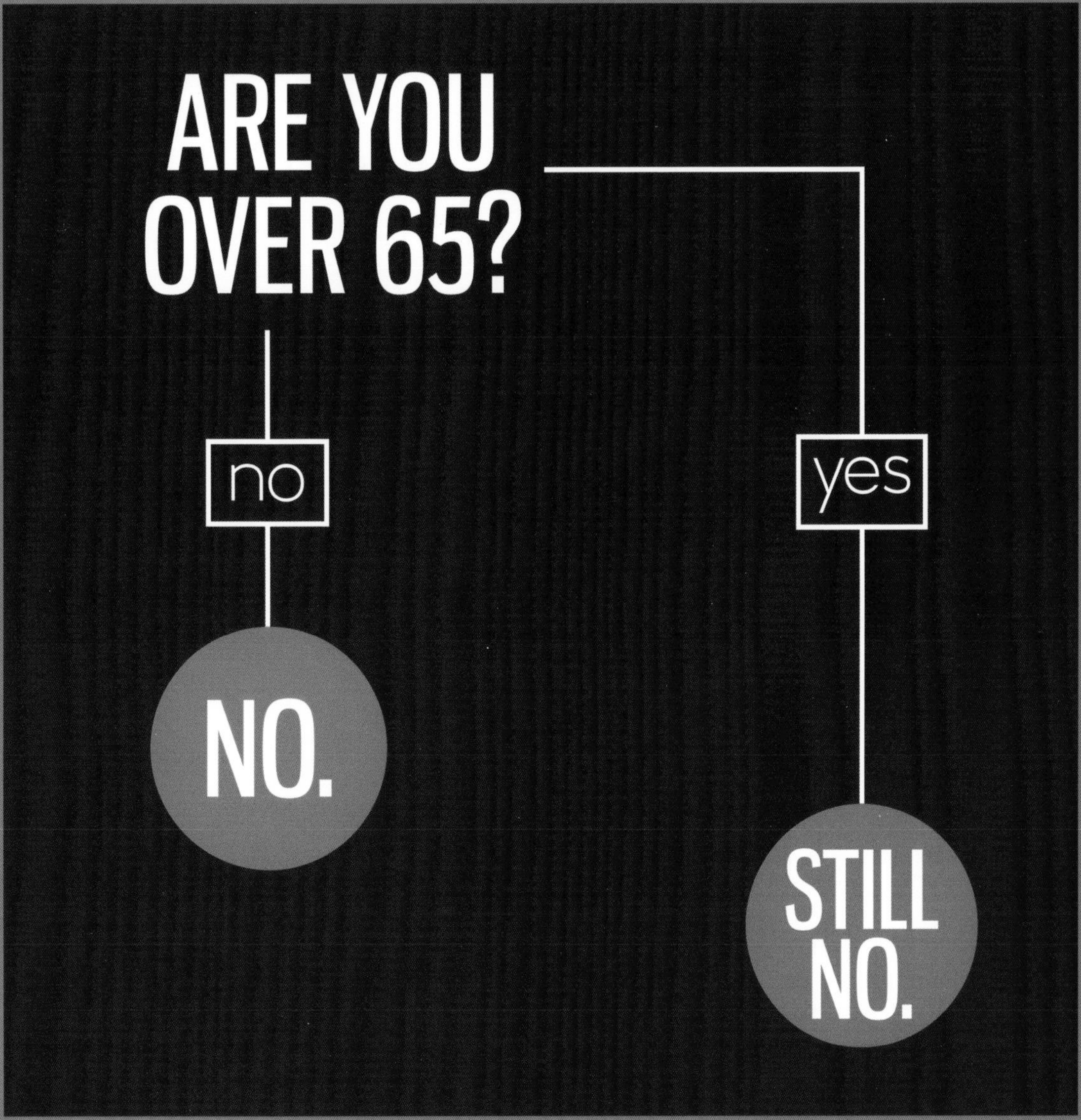

ARE YOU OVER 65?

no

NO.

yes

STILL NO.

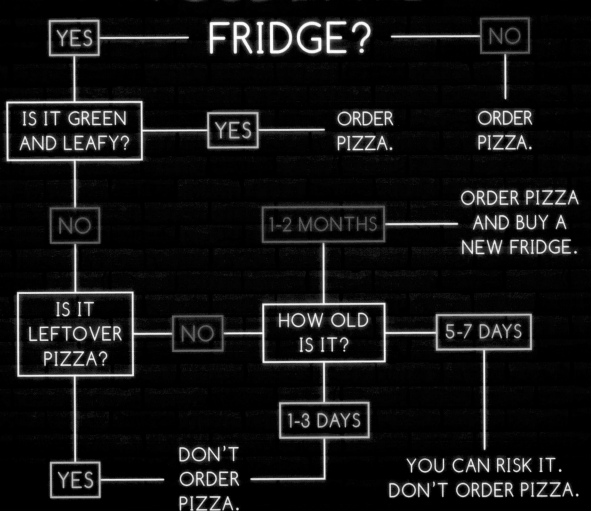

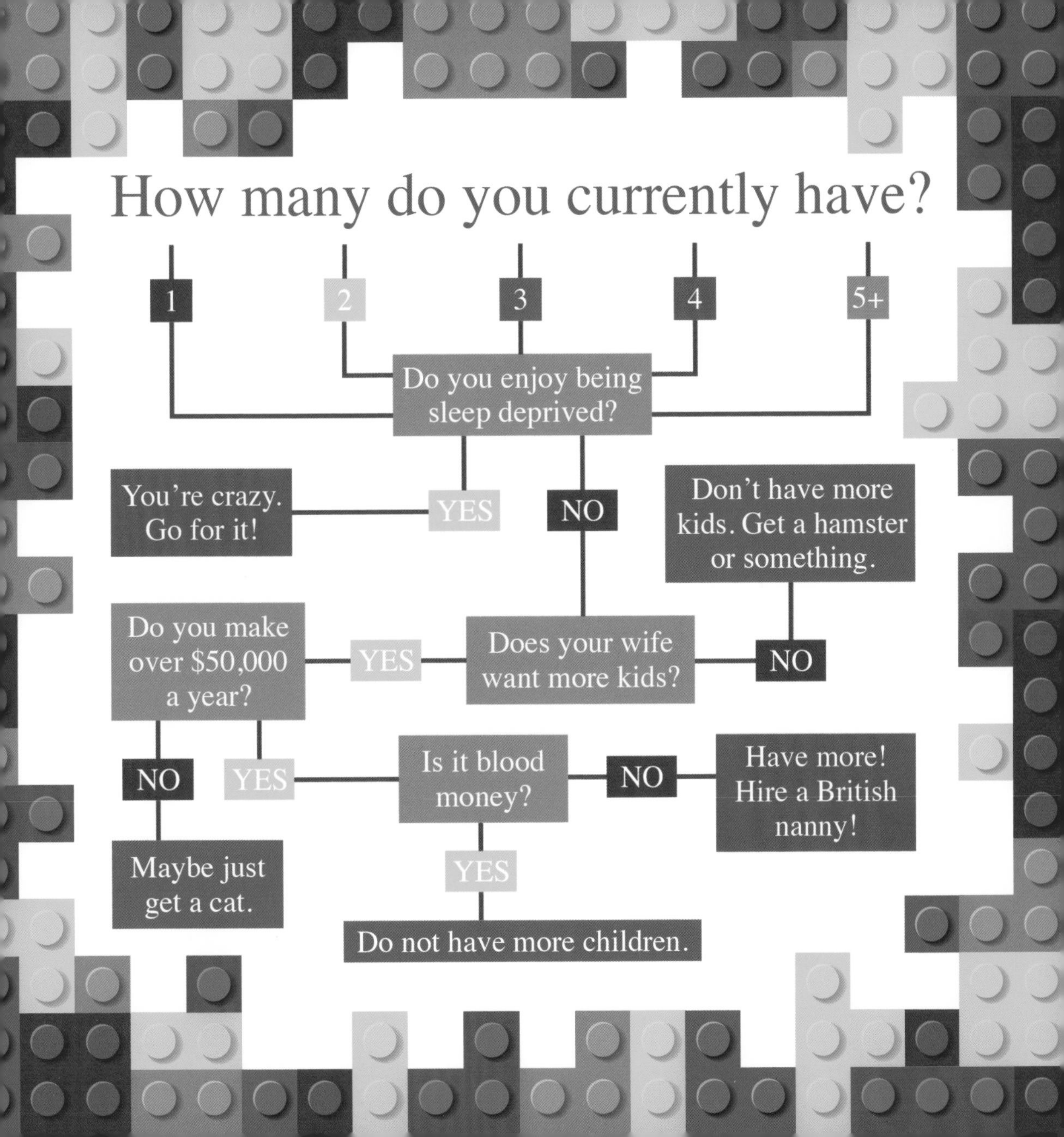

How many do you currently have?

1   **2**   **3**   **4**   **5+**

Do you enjoy being sleep deprived?

You're crazy. Go for it! ← YES | NO

Don't have more kids. Get a hamster or something.

Do you make over $50,000 a year? ← YES → Does your wife want more kids? → NO

NO | YES

Is it blood money? → NO → Have more! Hire a British nanny!

Maybe just get a cat.

YES

Do not have more children.

Should I
COACH MY KID'S SPORTS TEAM?

HAVE YOU MET THE BOY BEFORE?

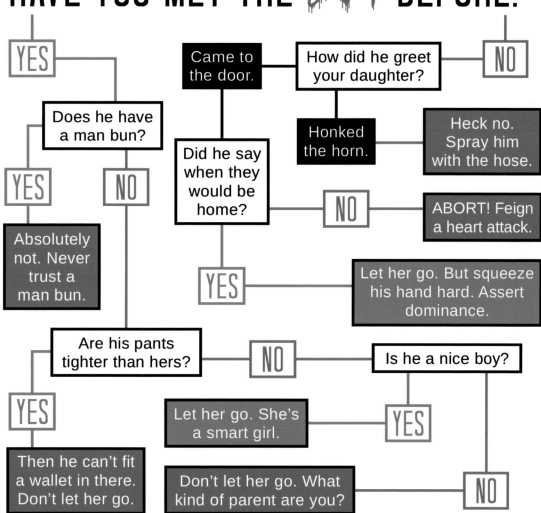

SHOULD I RUN A MARATHON?

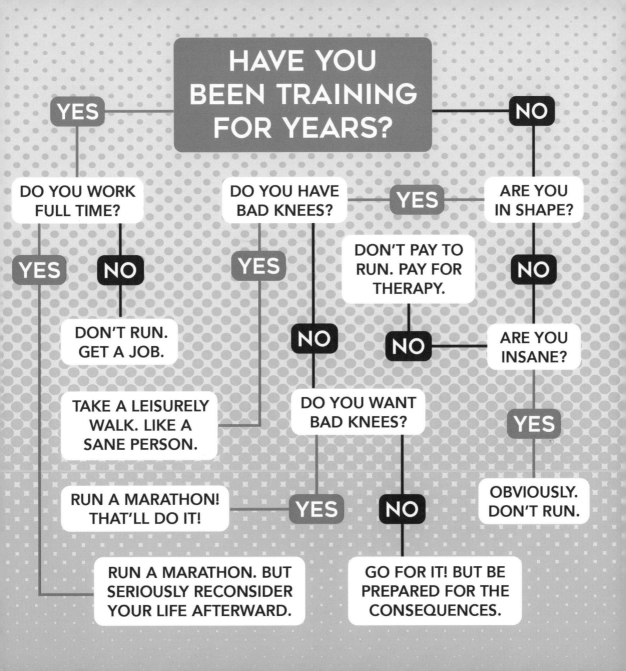

BY AIR MAIL

6c

WASHINGTON 5c

UNITED STATES

Should I write a letter?

APPROVED

PRIORITY MAIL

POST SERV
apr 23
12 AM
2013

AIR MAIL   AIR MAIL   AIR MAIL   AIR MAIL

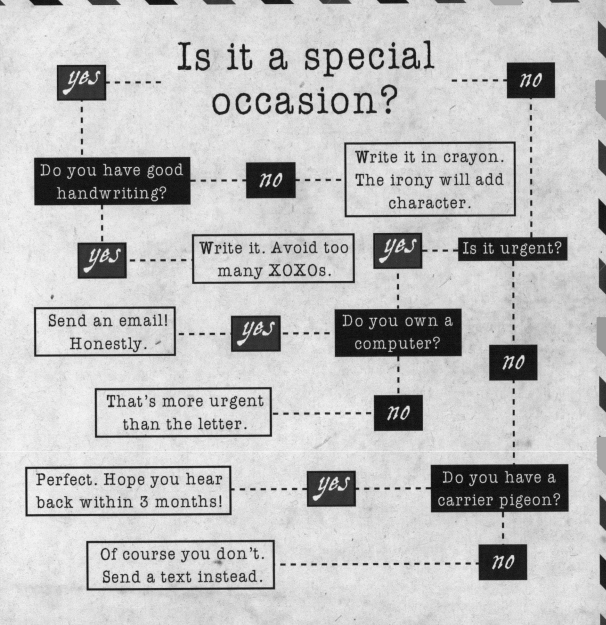

SHOULD I DRESS UP FOR

HALLOWEEN?

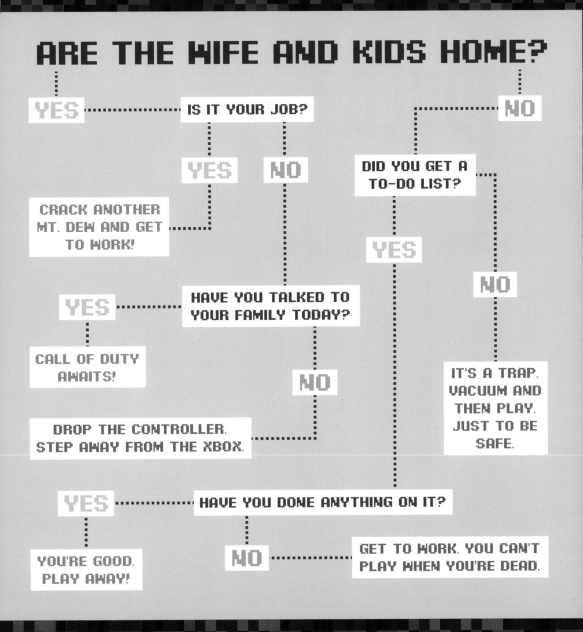

SHOULD I MOW THE LAWN?

SHOULD I GET MY KIDS A PET?

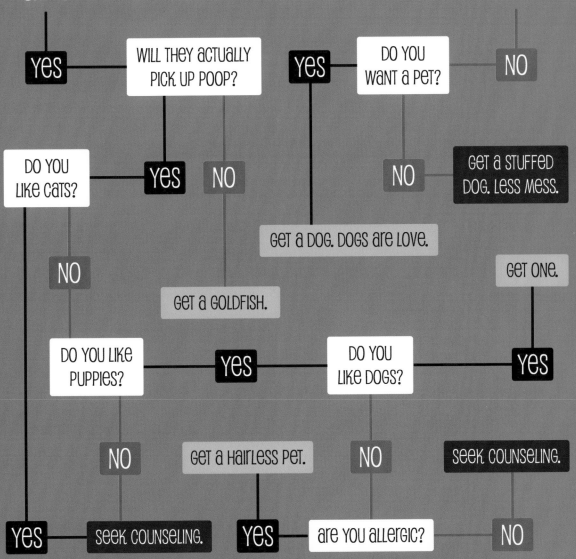

CERTIFICATE

OF OUTSTANDING ACHIEVEMENT

SHOULD I

Embarrass My Child?

CERTIFICATE AWARDED FOR

Flawless execution of fatherly duties including, but not limited to, playing princess songs while picking son up from school, telling dad jokes during dinner, cleaning shotgun while daughter gets ready for her first date, dancing in the middle of the grocery store, etc.

Today

DATE

Dad

RECIPIENT

HAVE THEY BEEN BAD LATELY?

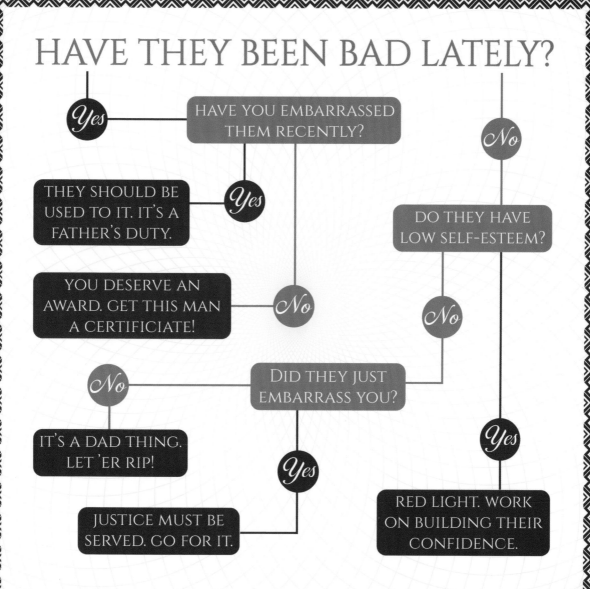

ARE YOU OVER 60?

YES

NO

You've lived this long. Do what you want.

Do you want to stay single? ···· **YES** ···· Are you single?

Carry on. Try Crocs. Go crazy! ···· **YES**

NO

YES

NO

No. Start small. Ditch the socks.

YES ···· Does your significant other like it?

Yes. Like any rational person, they'll run for the hills.

No. Burn them with fire.

Congrats on finding someone as crazy as you. Go for it!

NO

Do you enjoy being in a relationship?

YES

NO

SHOULD I TAKE MY KIDS TO THE PARK?

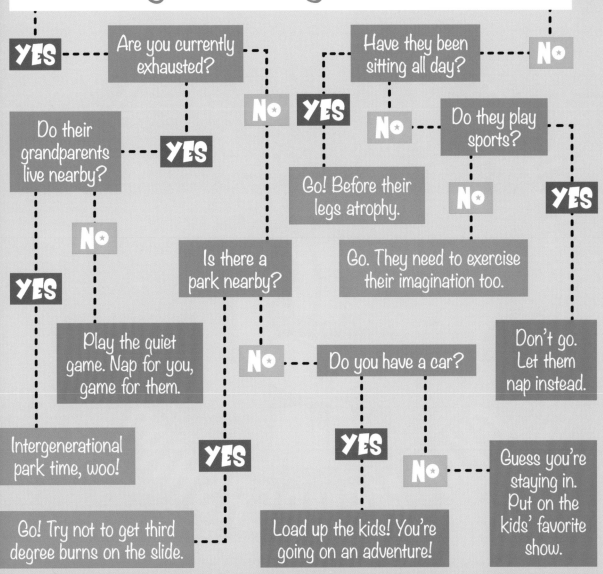

Are they bouncing off the walls?

YES — Are you currently exhausted?

Have they been sitting all day? — NO

NO

YES — YES

NO — Do they play sports?

Do their grandparents live nearby? — YES

Go! Before their legs atrophy.

NO — NO

YES

Go. They need to exercise their imagination too.

YES

Is there a park nearby?

Play the quiet game. Nap for you, game for them.

Don't go. Let them nap instead.

NO — Do you have a car?

Intergenerational park time, woo!

YES

YES

NO — Guess you're staying in. Put on the kids' favorite show.

Go! Try not to get third degree burns on the slide.

Load up the kids! You're going on an adventure!

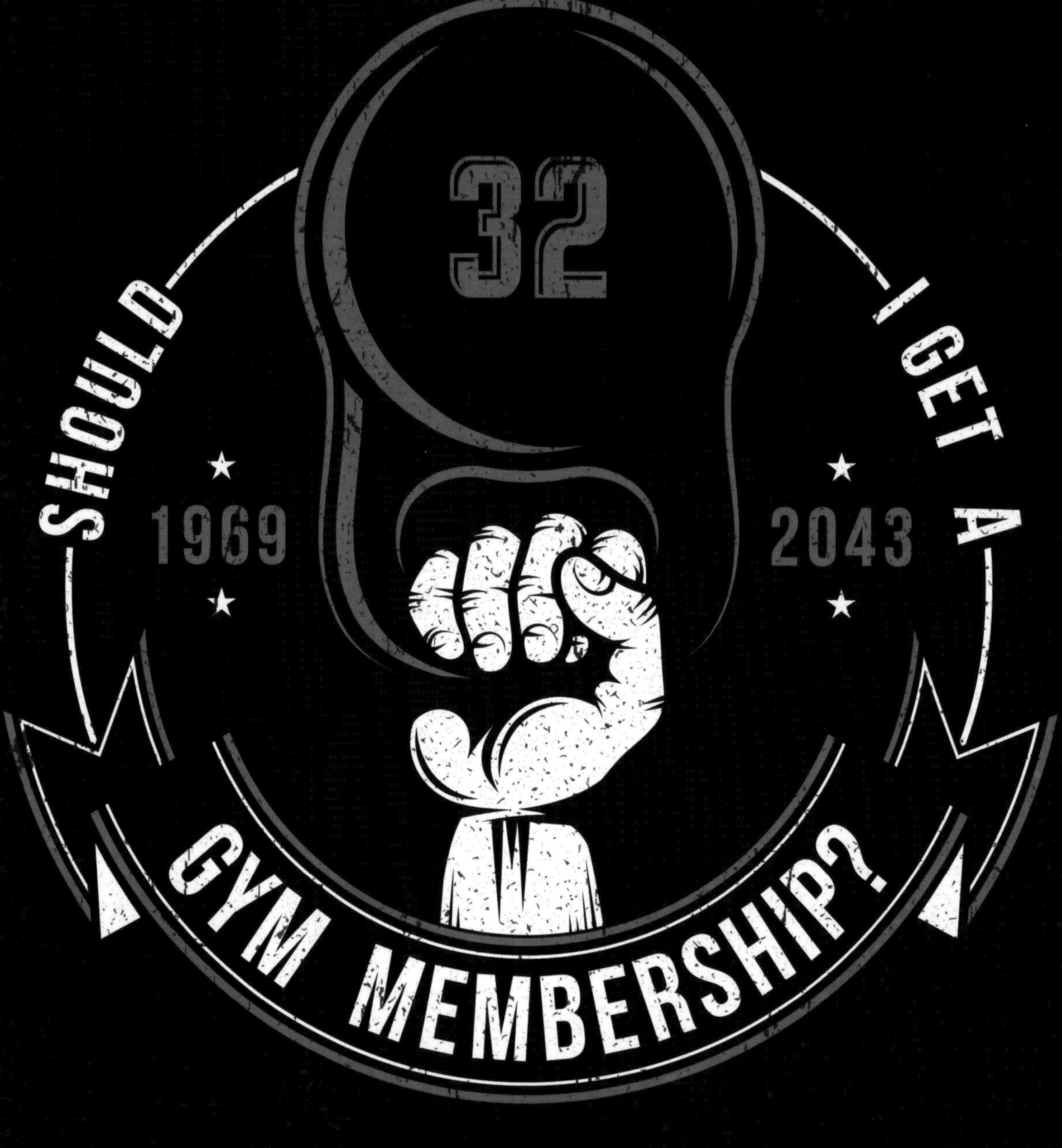
SHOULD
I GET A
32
1969
2043
GYM MEMBERSHIP?

DO MY KIDS NEED NEW SHOES?

SHOULD

I TAKE

MY FAMILY

ON A

PICNIC?

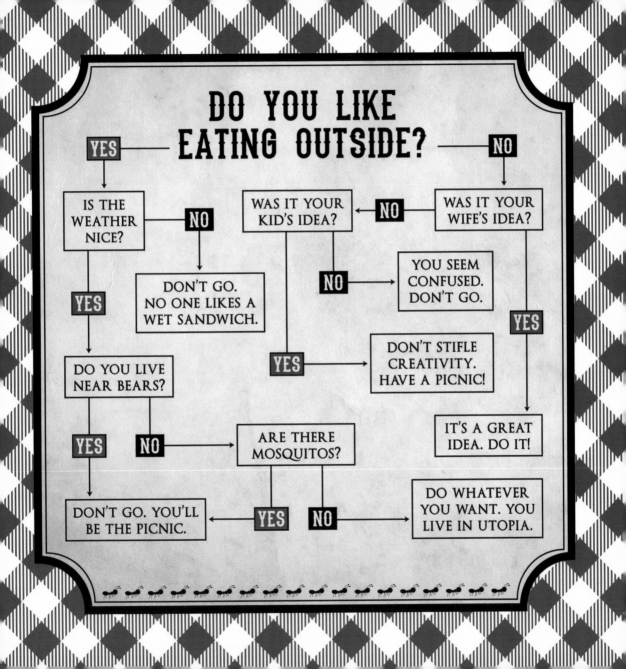

SHOULD I TAKE MY

FAMILY
WHITEWATER
RAFTING
THIS
SUMMER?

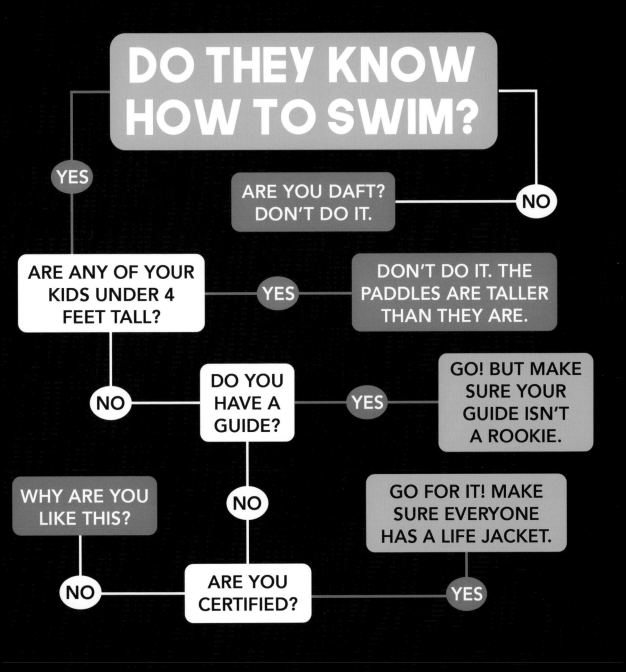

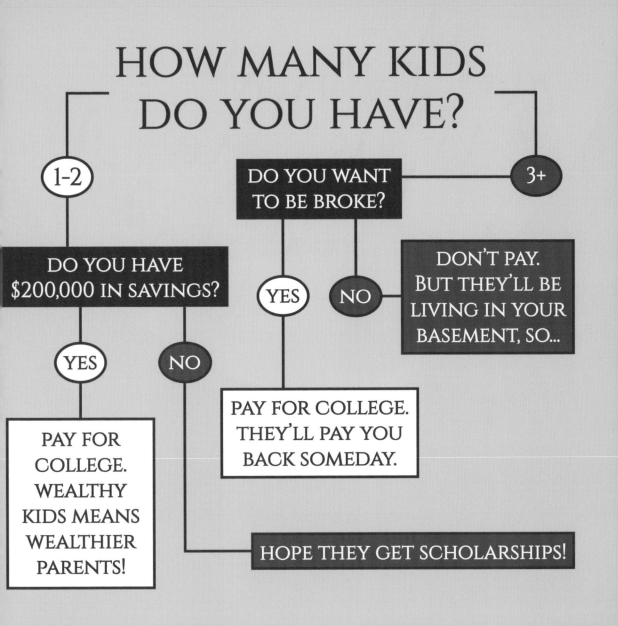

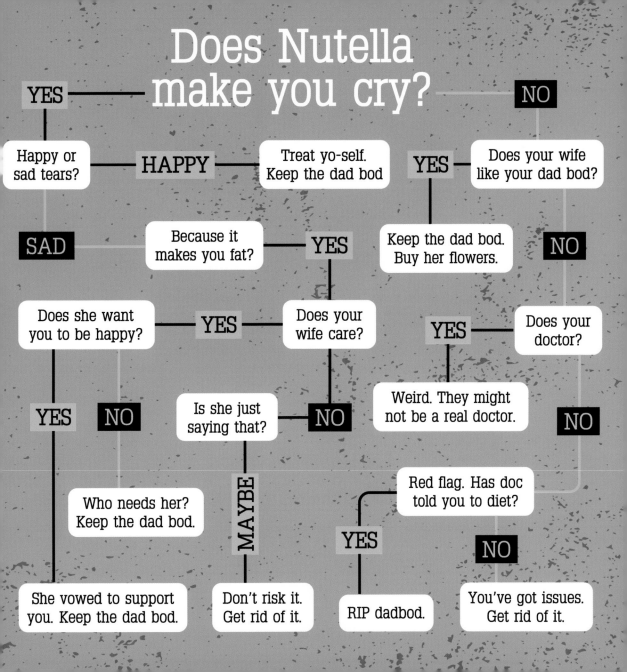

SHOULD I TAKE

My kids

TO THE

FAIR?

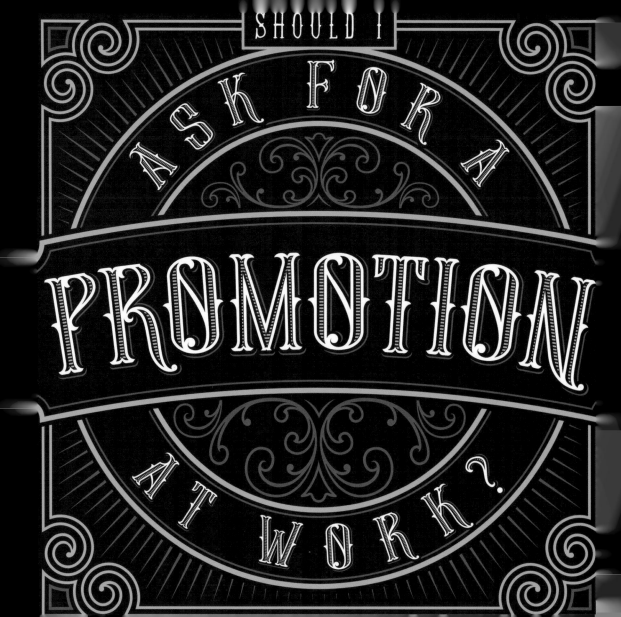

WHEN WAS YOUR LAST PROMOTION?

Never

Is it because you suck at your job?

YES — Why are you even asking?? Heck to the no!

NO — Is it because Brad stole it from you?

YES — You know what to do. Ex-Lax in his drink will teach him!

YES — Go for it. Go get that bread, dad!

NO — Well. Do you deserve it?

NO — Then get to work! Earn it, broseph!

Are you awesome at your job?

Last 2

YES — Secure the bag! Ask for that promotion!

NO — Do you just the least

YES — Eh, still worth it. Ask away!

N

How were you promoted in the first place? Don't ask!

DO I

NEED

GLASSES?

MCJFSB

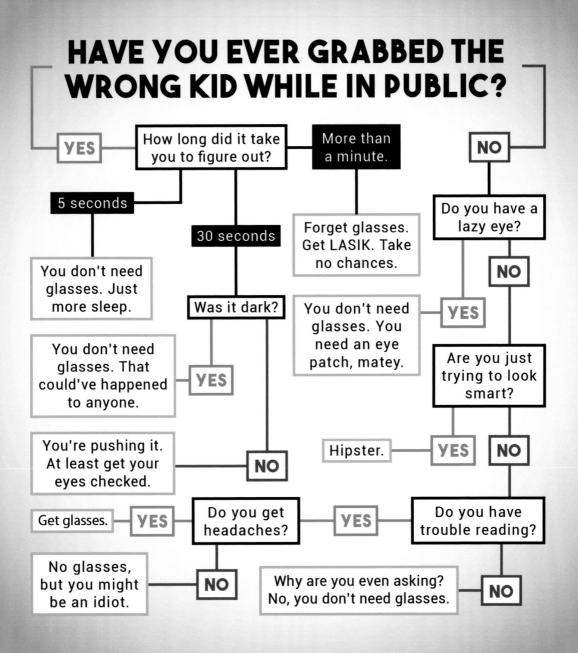

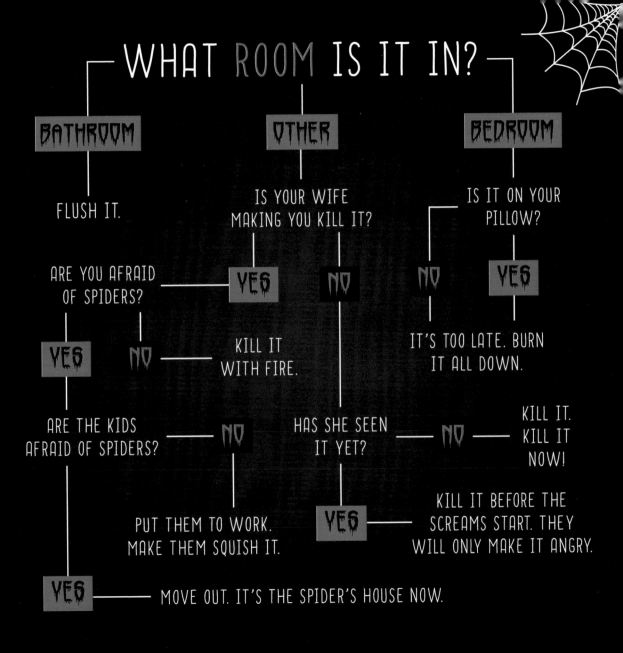

Can I RETIRE yet?

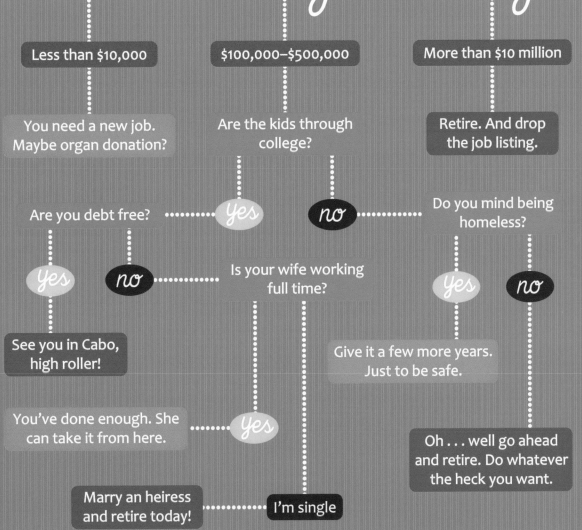

CAN I WEAR A **PLAID** SHIRT?

SHOULD I

LAUGH AT MY FATHER-IN-LAW?

DID HE TELL A JOKE?

YES — **NO**

WAS IT FUNNY? --- **NO**

YES --- **IS HE A COP?**

YES

N

COULD IT BE CONSIDERED OFFENSIVE?

PITY GIGGLE THEN CLAIM DIARRHEA AND ESCAPE.

COULD YOU TAKE HIM IN A FIGHT?

YES **NO**

DON'T LAUGH. HE HAS A GUN.

NO

IS YOUR WIFE AROUND? --- **NO**

LAUGH AND QUICKLY CHANGE THE SUBJECT.

DON'T LAUGH UNLESS YOU HAVE A DEATH WISH.

YES

LAUGH. THEN ACT HORRIFIED WHEN YOUR WIFE HEARS.

DON'T LAUGH AT ALL COSTS.

DON'T LAUGH. IT'S NOT WORTH SLEEPING ON THE COUCH.

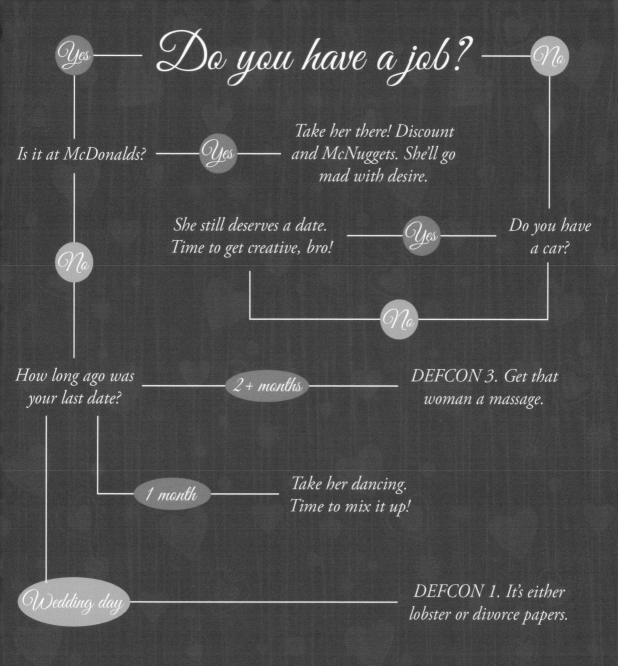

CAN I SKIP
the Family Reunion
THIS YEAR?

CAN I GO FISHING?

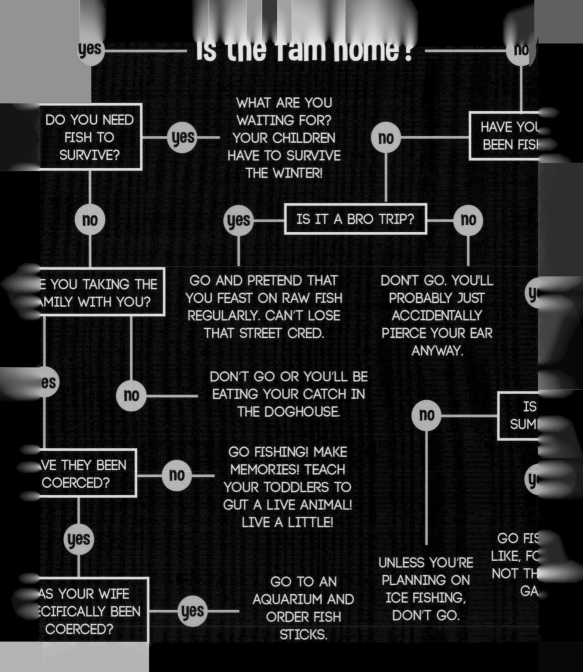

ABOUT THE AUTHOR
HEATH HARMISON

Being a superhero was always an ultimate dream of Heath's ...but due to his lack of athleticism, money, and tragic backstory, he decided that bringing laughter to the world would be the next best thing. He is a husband and father of two amazing kids, which is a great formula for great comedy. His observations of the struggles of fatherhood are hilarious and spot on. He's a full-time professional standup and improv comedian. His style of comedy kills in clubs, colleges, cruise ships, and festivals all over the world including the Fringe Festival in Edinburgh, Scotland. In the last 13 years, Heath has performed and traveled to over 22 different countries. He's traveled overseas to perform for the U.S. Troops in Iraq, Kuwait, and Abu Dhabi and performs regularly on the Las Vegas Strip at Planet Hollywood, The Tropicana, and the MGM Grand! He has worked with some of the best comics in the business including Brad Garrett, Louie Anderson, Dennis Miller, Eddie Griffin, and Roseanne Barr. His humor will burn images in your mind that will last weeks. For more laughs visit Heath's website at www.heathharmison.com.

STAND COMEDY SHOW